Steal not this book for fear of shame,
For in it is the owner's name;
And if this book you chance to borrow,
Return it promptly on the morrow.
Or when you die the Lord will say,
Where's that book you stole away?
And if you say you do not know,
The Lord will answer, Go below!

If this book should chance to roam —
Box its ears and send it home.

Black is the eye of the Raven,
Black is the eye of the Rook,
Black will be the eye of the Person,
Who tries to pinch this Book.

'And What,' Said the Emperor

'And what,' said the Emperor, 'does this poem describe?'
'It describes,' said the Poet, 'the cave of the Never-Never,
Would you like to see what's inside?' He offered his arm.
They stepped into the poem and disappeared forever.

George Barker

The New Oxford Treasury of Children's Poems

Surprise

The biggest
Surprise
On the library shelf
Is when you suddenly
Find yourself
Inside a book —
(The *hidden* you)

You wonder how
The author knew.

Beverly McLoughland

The New OXFORD
Treasury of
Children's Poems

Michael Harrison and
Christopher Stuart-Clark

OXFORD UNIVERSITY PRESS

OXFORD   NEW YORK   TORONTO

Contents

Alas! Alas! for Miss Mackay!

Alas! Alas! for Miss Mackay!
Her knives and forks have run away;
And when the cups and spoons are going,
She's sure there is no way of knowing.

Anon

The Man in the Wilderness

The man in the wilderness said to me,
'How many strawberries grow in the sea?'
I answered him as I thought good,
'As many red herrings as grow in the wood.'

Anon

There Was a Maid

There was a maid on Scrabble Hill,
And if not dead, she lives there still;
She grew so tall, she reached the sky,
And on the moon hung clothes to dry.

Anon

As I Was Going Up the Stair

As I was going up the stair
I met a man who wasn't there.
He wasn't there again today —
Oh, how I wish he'd go away.

Anon

Mary Went Down to Grandpa's Farm

Mary went down to Grandpa's farm;
The billy goat chased her round the barn,
Chased her up the sycamore tree,
And this is the song she sang to me:
'I like coffee, I like tea,
I like the boys and the boys like me.'

Anon

14

As I Looked Out

As I looked out on Saturday last,
A fat little pig went hurrying past,
Over his shoulder he wore a shawl,
Although it didn't seem cold at all.
I waved at him, but he didn't see,
For he never so much as looked at me.
Once again, when the moon was high,
I saw the little pig hurrying by;
Back he came at a terrible pace,
The moonlight shone on his little pink face,
And he smiled with a smile that was quite content,
But I never knew where that little pig went.

Anon

15

Twelve Huntsmen

Twelve huntsmen with horns and hounds,
Hunting over other men's grounds!
Eleven ships sailing o'er the main,
Some bound for France and some for Spain;
I wish them all safe home again.
Ten comets in the sky,
Some low and some high;
Nine peacocks in the air,
I wonder how they all came there,
I do not know and I do not care.
Eight joiners in a joiners' hall,
Working with the tools and all;
Seven lobsters in a dish,
As fresh as any heart could wish;
Six beetles against the wall,
Close by an old woman's apple stall;
Five puppies of our dog Ball,
Who daily for their breakfast call;
Four horses stuck in a bog,
Three monkeys tied to a clog;
Two pudding-ends would choke a dog,
With a gaping wide-mouthed waddling frog.

Anon

The Thief and the Shepherd

'Shepherdy, Shepherdy, count your sheep.'

'I can't come now, I'm fast asleep.'

'If you don't come now, they'll all be gone,
So Shepherdy, Shepherdy, come along.'

Anon

Lullaby

Hush, little baby, don't say a word,
Papa's going to buy you a mocking bird.

If the mocking bird won't sing,
Papa's going to buy you a diamond ring.

If the diamond ring turns to brass,
Papa's going to buy you a looking-glass.

If the looking-glass gets broke,
Papa's going to buy you a billy-goat.

If that billy-goat runs away,
Papa's going to buy you another today.

Anon

How Many Miles to Babylon?

How many miles to Babylon?
Three-score and ten.
Can I get there by candle-light?
Yes, and back again.

Anon

Lullaby

A heart to hate you
Is as far away as the moon.
A heart to love you
Is as close as the door.

Barundi

A Cradle Song

Golden slumbers kiss your eyes,
Smiles awake you when you rise.
Sleep, pretty wantons, do not cry,
And I will sing a lullaby:
Rock them, rock them, lullaby.

Care is heavy, therefore sleep you;
You are care, and care must keep you.
Sleep, pretty wantons, do not cry,
And I will sing a lullaby:
Rock them, rock them, lullaby.

Thomas Dekker

Tumbling

In jumping and tumbling
  We spend the whole day,
Till night by arriving
  Has finished our play.

What then? One and all,
  There's no more to be said,
As we tumbled all day,
  So we tumble to bed.

Anon

20

The Dustman

When the shades of night are falling, and the sun goes down,
O! the Dustman comes a-creeping in from Shut-eye Town.
And he throws dust in the eyes of all the babies that he meets,
No matter where he finds them, in the house or in the streets.
Then the babies' eyes grow heavy and the lids drop down,
When the Dustman comes a-creeping in from Shut-eye Town.

When mother lights the lamp and draws the curtains down,
O! the Dustman comes a-creeping in from Shut-eye Town,
And the babies think the Dustman is as mean as he can be,
For he shuts their eyes at nightfall, just when they want to see.
But their little limbs are weary, for all they fret and frown,
When the Dustman comes a-creeping in from Shut-eye Town.

Anon

Night-Lights

There is no need to light a night-light
On a light night like tonight;
For a night-light's light's a slight light
When the moonlight's white and bright.

Anon

Z

Zebediah Zidcup
  Puzzles in his head
Round and round and round they go
  When he lies in bed

Zebediah Zidcup
  Looking at the moon
Round and round and round it goes
  Likewise does the sun

Likewise do the elephants
  Likewise do the sheep
Round and round and round they go
  Till they fall asleep

Cara Lockhart Smith

Adam and Eve and Pinchme

Adam and Eve and Pinchme
Went down to the river to bathe.
Adam and Eve were drowned —
Who do you think was saved?

Anon

As I Was Going Out One Day

As I was going out one day
My head fell off and rolled away.
But when I saw that it was gone,
I picked it up and put it on.

And when I got into the street
A fellow cried: 'Look at your feet!'
I looked at them and sadly said:
'I've left them both asleep in bed!'

Anon

The Land of Nod

From breakfast on through all the day
At home among my friends I stay;
But every night I go abroad
Afar into the Land of Nod.

All by myself I have to go,
With none to tell me what to do —
All alone beside the streams
And up the mountain-sides of dreams.

The strangest things are there for me,
Both things to eat and things to see,
And many frightening sights abroad
Till morning in the Land of Nod.

Try as I like to find the way,
I never can get back by day,
Nor can remember plain and clear
The curious music that I hear.

Robert Louis Stevenson

Topsy-Turvy Land

The people walk upon their heads,
The sea is made of sand,
The children go to school by night,
In Topsy-Turvy Land.

The front-door step is at the back,
You're walking when you stand,
You wear your hat upon your feet,
In Topsy-Turvy Land.

And buses on the sea you'll meet,
While pleasure boats are planned
To travel up and down the streets
Of Topsy-Turvy Land.

You pay for what you never get,
I think it must be grand,
For when you go you're coming back,
In Topsy-Turvy Land.

H. E. Wilkinson

What's in There?

What's in there?
  Gold and money.
Where's my share of it?
  The mouse ran away with it.
Where's the mouse?
  In her house.

Where's the house?
  In the wood.
Where's the wood?
  The fire burnt it.
Where's the fire?
  The water quenched it.

Where's the water?
  The brown bull drank it.
Where's the brown bull?
  At the back of Birnie's Hill.
Where's Birnie's Hill?
  All clad with snow.
Where's the snow?
  The sun melted it.
Where's the sun?
  High, high up in the air.

Anon

If

If all the seas were one sea,
What a *great* sea that would be!
If all the trees were one tree,
What a *great* tree that would be!
And if all the axes were one axe,
What a *great* axe that would be!
And if all the men were one man,
What a *great* man that would be!
And if the *great* man took the *great* axe,
And cut down the *great* tree,
And let it fall into the *great* sea,
What a splish-splash that would be!

Anon

The Old Man's Toes

Up the street,
Down the street,
My
            Joan
                    goes —
(Mind you don't tread upon the
Old
            Man's
                    Toes!)
She hops along the pavement
Into every Square,
But she mustn't touch the Cracks in
    between
Them
            There.
The Squares on the pavement
Are safe
            as can
                    be:
One is the Sands
By the side
            of the
                    sea;
One is a Garden where
Joan's
            flowers
                    grow;
One is a Meadow
She
        and I
            know.

But the Cracks are *dangerous*,
As
        Everybody
                knows!
The Cracks in the Pavement are the
Old
        Man's
                Toes.

Any one who treads on the
Old
        Man's
                Corn
Will wish in a jiffy he had
Never
        been
                born!
For the Sea will roll up and
Suck
        you
            down!
And a horrid blight will turn your
Garden
            brown!
And into the Meadow with an
Angry
            Moo
A Big Cross Cow will come
Rushing
        at
            You!

Up the street and down the street
My
    Joan
        goes —
Here she makes a Pudding,
There she smells a Rose,
Yonder she goes stooping where the
Mushroom
        grows —
(Mind, Joan! don't tread upon the
Old
    Man's
        Toes!)

Eleanor Farjeon

You, North Must Go

You, North must go,
To a hut of snow;
You, South in a trice,
To an island of spice;
You, off to China,
And sit on a hill!
And you to that chair,
And be five minutes still!

Anon

Sally's Alphabet

A is for alphabet
B is for boy
C is for cat, if you like

but cats can't learn letters
and all boys enjoy
racing downhill on a bike

D is for donkey
E is for egg
F is a fairly big fish

but donkeys don't swim
and a fish wouldn't eat
two hard-boiled eggs on a dish

G is a girl, and
Home is a place
I is for ink, I should think

but girls who go home
with ink on their face
must scrub themselves clean in the sink

J is for Jennifer
K is for King
L is a lizard that's green

so Jennifer once
took her lizard along
to wave at the King and the Queen

M is a mouse
N is a newt
O is an ostrich, for sure

they live in a house
where they sing to a flute
as they sit in a ring on the floor

P is for pepper
Q is a queue
R is a big roundabout

but pepper could make
a whole queue go 'Atchoo!'
and rush round and round to get out

S is a suit, and
T is a tailor
U is an uncle who's old

    he went off to bed
    with a needle and thread
    to sew up some cloth made of gold

V is a vegetable
W a whale
X is a kind of a cross

    but whales who eat vegetables
    with a big meal
    get pains as they pitch and they toss

Y is a yawn
Z is zigzag
A takes us back to the start

    and you're yawning, my love
    as you zigzag to bed
    so Goodnight and God bless you, sweetheart

Edwin Brock

The Table and the Chair

Said the Table to the Chair,
'You can hardly be aware,
How I suffer from the heat,
And the chilblains on my feet!
If we took a little walk,
We might have a little talk!
Pray let us take the air!'
Said the Table to the Chair.

Said the Chair unto the Table,
'Now you know we are not able!
How foolishly you talk,
When you know we cannot walk!'
Said the Table, with a sigh,
'It can do no harm to try,
I've as many legs as you,
Why can't we walk on two?'

So they both went slowly down,
And walked about the town
With a cheerful bumpy sound,
As they toddled round and round.
And everybody cried,
As they hastened to their side,
'See! the Table and the Chair
Have come out to take the air!'

But in going down an alley,
To a castle in a valley,
They completely lost their way,
And wandered all the day,
Till, to see them safely back,
They paid a Ducky-quack,
And a Beetle, and a Mouse,
Who took them to their house.

Then they whispered to each other,
'O delightful little brother!
What a lovely walk we've taken!
Let us dine on Beans and Bacon!'
So the Ducky, and the leetle
Browny-Mousy and the Beetle
Dined, and danced upon their heads
Till they toddled to their beds.

Edward Lear

Catch a Little Rhyme

Once upon a time
I caught a little rhyme

I set it on the floor
but it ran right out the door

I chased it on my bicycle
but it melted to an icicle

I scooped it up in my hat
but it turned into a cat

I caught it by the tail
but it stretched into a whale

I followed it in a boat
but it changed into a goat

When I fed it tin and paper
it became a tall skyscraper

Then it grew into a kite
and flew far out of sight . . .

Eve Merriam

The Sound Collector

A stranger called this morning
Dressed all in black and grey
Put every sound into a bag
And carried them away

The whistling of the kettle
The turning of the lock
The purring of the kitten
The ticking of the clock

The popping of the toaster
The crunching of the flakes
When you spread the marmalade
The scraping noise it makes

The hissing of the frying-pan
The ticking of the grill
The bubbling of the bathtub
As it starts to fill

The drumming of the raindrops
On the window-pane
When you do the washing-up
The gurgle of the drain

The crying of the baby
The squeaking of the chair
The swishing of the curtain
The creaking of the stair

A stranger called this morning
He didn't leave his name
Left us only silence
Life will never be the same.

Roger McGough

I am the Song

I am the song that sings the bird.
I am the leaf that grows the land.
I am the tide that moves the moon.
I am the stream that halts the sand.
I am the cloud that drives the storm.
I am the earth that lights the sun.
I am the fire that strikes the stone.
I am the clay that shapes the hand.
I am the word that speaks the man.

Charles Causley

Give Me Your Name!

Give me your name, and I will . . .

whisper it into the forests,
spell it out in the sands,
I'll shout it over the thunder,
breathe it away on the wind.
I'll spill it over the mountains,
let it echo through the rain;
I'll sing it into a seashell,
if you give me your name.

Judith Nicholls

The Piper

Piping down the valleys wild,
  Piping songs of pleasant glee,
On a cloud I saw a child,
  And he, laughing, said to me,

'Pipe a song about a lamb,'
  So I piped with merry cheer;
'Piper, pipe that song again,'
  So I piped, he wept to hear.

'Drop thy pipe, thy happy pipe,
  Sing thy songs of happy cheer.'
So I sang the same again,
  While he wept with joy to hear.

'Piper, sit thee down and write
  In a book that all may read.'
So he vanish'd from my sight;
  And I pluck'd a hollow reed,

And I made a rural pen,
  And I stained the water clear,
And I wrote my happy songs
  Every child may joy to hear.

William Blake

When I Was Christened

When I was christened
they held me up
and poured some water
out of a cup.

The trouble was
it fell on me,
and I and water
don't agree.

A lot of christeners
stood and listened:
I let them know
that I was christened.

David McCord

New Baby

My baby brother makes so much noise
that the Rottweiler next door
phoned up to complain.

My baby brother makes so much noise
that all the big green frogs
came out the drains.

My baby brother makes so much noise
that the rats and the mice
wore headphones.

My baby brother makes so much noise
that I can't ask my mum a question,
so much noise that sometimes

I think of sitting the cat on top of him
in his pretty little cot with all his teddies.
But even the cat is terrified of his cries.

So I have devised a plan. A soundproof room.
A telephone to talk to my mum.
A small lift to receive food and toys.

Thing is, it will cost a fortune.
The other thing is, the frogs have gone.
It's not bad now. Not that I like him or anything.

Jackie Kay

Little

I am the sister of him
And he is my brother.
He is too little for us
To talk to each other.

So every morning I show him
My doll and my book;
But every morning he still is
Too little to look.

Dorothy Aldis

I'm the Youngest
in Our House

I'm the youngest in our house
so it goes like this:

My brother comes in and says:
'Tell him to clear the fluff
out from under his bed.'
Mum says,
'Clear the fluff
out from under your bed.'
Father says,
'You heard what your mother said.'
'What?' I say.
'The fluff,' he says.

'Clear the fluff
out from under your bed.'
So I say,
'There's fluff under his bed, too,
you know.'
So Father says,
'But we're talking about the fluff
under *your* bed.'
'You will clear it up
won't you?' Mum says.
So now my brother — all puffed up —
says,
'Clear the fluff
out from under your bed,
clear the fluff
out from under your bed.'
Now I'm angry. I am angry.
So I say — what shall I say?
I say,
'Shuttup, stinks
YOU CAN'T RULE MY LIFE.'

Michael Rosen

45

The Whistler

My little brother is almost six,
He's good at maths and magic tricks,
He's quite a neat writer,
He can hop and jump and pull funny faces,
He can do top buttons and tie his laces,
He's a fearless fighter.

But he wanted to whistle — and though he tried
Till his face went red and he almost cried,
He still couldn't do it,
So he asked me how and I said: 'Make an O
With your mouth and then, very gently, blow
A whistle through it.'

And he did — but now the trouble is
My little brother practises
All day long,
He sucks in his cheeks, he puffs and blows,
Whatever he's doing, his whistling goes
On and on . . . and on . . .

June Crebbin

poem for rodney

people always ask what
am i going to be
when i grow
up and i always
just think
i'd like to grow
up

Nikki Giovanni

I'm Just Going Out

I'm just going out for a moment.

Why?

To make a cup of tea.

Why?

Because I'm thirsty.

Why?

Because it's hot.

Why?

Because the sun's shining.

Why?

Because it's summer.

Why?

Because that's when it is.

Why?

Why don't you stop saying why?

Why?

Tea-time why.
High-time-you-stopped-saying-why-time.

What?

Michael Rosen

Ask Mummy Ask Daddy

When I ask Daddy
Daddy says ask Mummy

When I ask Mummy
Mummy says ask Daddy.
I don't know where to go.

Better ask my teddy
he never says no.

John Agard

My Dad, Your Dad

My dad's fatter than your dad,
Yes, my dad's fatter than yours:
If he eats any more he won't fit in the house,
He'll have to live out of doors.

Yes, but my dad's balder than your dad,
My dad's balder, OK,
He's only got two hairs left on his head
And both are turning grey.

Ah, but my dad's thicker than your dad,
My dad's thicker, all right.
He has to look at his watch to see
If it's noon or the middle of the night.

Yes, but my dad's more boring than your dad.
If he ever starts counting sheep
When he can't get to sleep at night, he finds
It's the sheep that go to sleep.

But my dad doesn't mind your dad.
Mine quite likes yours too.
I suppose they don't always think much of US!
That's true, I suppose, that's true.

Kit Wright

50

Going Hairless

Oh, Dad, why did you do it?
It's just — you look so weird,
Your face looks sort of lonely
Without its fuzzy beard.

I liked your face as it was, Dad,
I liked it covered in hair,
I liked your chin all bristly
Not pink and bald and bare.

Why did you shave it off, Dad?
It doesn't look like you,
Your lips look sort of worried
And not sure what to do.

I'll miss your tickly beard, Dad,
When you come to say goodnight,
I'll miss the way that it prickles
Whenever we have a fight.

My friends all liked your beard, Dad,
I know they'll miss it too,
I'm not sure that they'll recognize
That you are really you.

I bet if you started today, Dad,
It wouldn't take long, I'm sure,
For your beard to be back to normal,
And you'd be my dad once more.

June Crebbin

Two of Everything

My friend Shola said to me that she said to her mum:
'It's not fair, Carla (that's me) has two of everything:

Carla has two bedrooms,
two sets of toys, two telephones,

two wardrobes, two door mats,
two mummies, two cats,

two water purifiers, two kitchens,
two environmentally friendly squeezies.'

My friend Shola said to me that she said to her mum:
'Why can't you and Dad get divorced?'

But the thing Shola doesn't even realize yet,
is that there are two of me.

Jackie Kay

Everybody

She's good at everything
And everybody says she is.

I'm good for nothing
And you keep on telling me.

I wish you'd sometimes say
I'm good at something.

It's not my fault I don't like
Anything she's good at.

Why do you keep on telling me
What everybody says?

Who is everybody anyway?
It's all your fault.

John Mole

Sometimes

Sometimes I share things,
And everyone says
'Isn't it lovely? Isn't it fine?'

I give my little brother
Half my ice-cream cone
And let him play
With toys that are mine.

But today
I don't feel like sharing.
Today
I want to be let alone.
Today
I don't want to give my little brother
A single thing except
A shove.

Eve Merriam

The Quarrel

I quarrelled with my brother
I don't know what about,
One thing led to another
And somehow we fell out.
The start of it was slight,
The end of it was strong,
He said he was right,
I knew he was wrong!

We hated one another.
The afternoon turned black.
Then suddenly my brother
Thumped me on the back,
And said, 'Oh, *come* along!
We can't go on all night —
I was in the wrong.'
So he was in the right.

Eleanor Farjeon

Matilda

Who told Lies, and was Burned to Death

Matilda told such dreadful lies,
It made one gasp and stretch one's eyes;
Her aunt, who, from her earliest youth,
Had kept a strict regard for truth,
Attempted to believe Matilda:
The effort very nearly killed her,
And would have done so, had not she
Discovered this infirmity.

For once, towards the close of day,
Matilda, growing tired of play,
And finding she was left alone,
Went tiptoe to the telephone
And summoned the immediate aid
Of London's noble fire-brigade.
Within an hour the gallant band
Were pouring in on every hand,
From Putney, Hackney Downs, and Bow
With courage high and hearts a-glow
They galloped, roaring through the town,
'Matilda's house is burning down!'
Inspired by British cheers and loud
Proceeding from the frenzied crowd,
They ran their ladders through a score
Of windows on the ballroom floor;
And took peculiar pains to souse
The pictures up and down the house,
Until Matilda's aunt succeeded
In showing them they were not needed;
And even then she had to pay
To get the men to go away!

It happened that a few weeks later
Her aunt was off to the theatre
To see that interesting play
The Second Mrs Tanqueray,
She had refused to take her niece
To hear this entertaining piece:
A deprivation just and wise
To punish her for telling lies.
That night a fire *did* break out —
You should have heard Matilda shout!
You should have heard her scream and bawl,
And throw the window up and call
To people passing in the street —
(The rapidly increasing heat
Encouraging her to obtain
Their confidence) — but all in vain!
For every time she shouted 'Fire!'
They only answered 'Little liar!'
And therefore when her aunt returned,
Matilda, and the house, were burned.

Hilaire Belloc

Whisper Whisper

whisper whisper
whisper whisper
goes my sister
down the phone

whisper whisper
go the beech leaves
breathing in the
wind alone

whisper whisper
whisper whisper
slips the river
on the stone

whisper whisper
go my parents
when they whisper
on their own

I don't mind the
whisper whisper
whisper whisper
it's a tune

sometimes though
I wish the whisper
whisperings would
shut up soon

Kit Wright

The Silence

It wasn't your fault,
It was just the way
That things turned out
And I don't know why.

Nobody meant it
Whatever it was
That started the silence
All over our house.

Please don't go
But if you must
Then think of us sometimes.
You're the best.

Send me a postcard
(*Wish you were here*)
And I'll believe you
Wherever you are.

Perhaps before long
The silence will break.
Everyone's waiting
For you to speak.

John Mole

Teabag

I'd like to be a teabag,
and stay at home all day
and talk to other teabags
in a teabag sort of way.

I'd love to be a teabag,
and lie in a little box
and never have to wash my face
or change my dirty socks.

I'd like to be a Tetley bag,
an Earl Grey one perhaps,
and doze all day and lie around
with Earl Grey kind of chaps.

I wouldn't have to do a thing,
no homework, jobs or chores —
just lie inside a comfy box
of teabags and their snores.

I wouldn't have to do exams,
I needn't tidy rooms,
or sweep the floor, or feed the cat
or wash up all the spoons.

I wouldn't have to do a thing —
A life of bliss, you see . . .
except that once in all my life

   I'd make a cup of tea.

Peter Dixon

Dog's Dinner

On Thursday night
my mother said
that I could sleep
in the barley-sugar bed.

I dreamed of sailing
a bubble-gum boat
blown big as a dinosaur
to keep me afloat.

On Friday night
my mother said
my sister could sleep
in the barley-sugar bed.

She dreamed of
a liquorice homework book
that ate the sums
when she was stuck.

On Saturday
my mother said
she would like to sleep
in the barley-sugar bed.

She dreamed of
a trifle covered in cream
with lollipop spoons
to lick it clean.

When Sunday came
my mother said
the dog could sleep
on the barley-sugar bed.

He ate it.

Irene Rawnsley

Quieter than Snow

I went to school a day too soon
And couldn't understand
Why silence hung in the yard like sheets
Nothing to flap or spin, no creaks
Or shocks of voices, only air.

And the car-park empty of teachers' cars
Only the first September leaves
Dropping like paper. No racks of bikes
No kicking legs, no fights,
No voices, laughter, anything.

Yet the door was open. My feet
Sucked down the corridor. My reflection
Walked with me past the hall.
My classroom smelt of nothing. And the silence
Rolled like thunder in my ears.

At every desk a still child stared at me
Teachers walked through walls and back again
Cupboard doors swung open, and out crept
More silent children, and still more.

They tiptoed round me
Touched me with ice-cold hands
And opened up their mouths with laughter
That was

Quieter than snow.

Berlie Doherty

First Day Back

It seems to me since time began,
It seems to be the rule,
That every teacher has to say,
First day back at school:

'What did you do in the holidays?
Write as much as you can,
Did you travel abroad this year
Or stay in a caravan?

Did you visit a stately home
Or walk in the countryside?
Remember to put in the details
So that I know you've tried.

Perhaps you went to the seaside,
Perhaps you stayed with Gran,
We'll call it "Holiday Memories" — now
Write as much as you can.'

Same old thing, year in year out,
And everybody knows
We'll have to write at least a page
Oh well, eyes down, here goes . . .

June Crebbin

Playgrounds

Playgrounds are such gobby places.
Know what I mean?
Everyone seems to have something to
Talk about, giggle, whisper, scream and shout about,
I mean, it's like being in a parrot cage.

And playgrounds are such pushy places.
Know what I mean?
Everyone seems to have to
Run about, jump, kick, do cartwheels, handstands, fly around,
I mean, it's like being inside a whirlwind.

And playgrounds are such patchy places.
Know what I mean?
Everyone seems to
Go round in circles, lines and triangles, coloured shapes,
I mean, it's like being in a kaleidoscope.

And playgrounds are such pally places.
Know what I mean?
Everyone seems to
Have best friends, secrets, link arms, be in gangs.
Everyone, except me.

Know what I mean?

Berlie Doherty

Growing Cress in a Polystyrene Trough

A polystyrene trough
Keeps seeds warm
And its thick white walls
Keep them from harm.

The cress seeds we planted
Were small as pencil dots
Spattering the soil
We put in the trough.

It took only two weeks
For them to grow
Into a thick green forest
In walls as white as snow.

Stanley Cook

from 'Arithmetic'

Arithmetic is where numbers fly
   like pigeons in and out of your head.
Arithmetic tells you how many you lose or win
   if you know how many you had
   before you lost or won.
Arithmetic is seven eleven all good children
   go to heaven — or five six bundle of sticks.
Arithmetic is numbers you squeeze from your
   head to your hand to your pencil to your paper
   till you get the right answer . . .
If you have two animal crackers, one good and one bad,
   and you eat one and a striped zebra
   with streaks all over him eats the other,
   how many animal crackers will you have
   if somebody offers you five six seven and you say
   No no no and you say Nay nay nay
   and you say Nix nix nix?
If you ask your mother for one fried egg
   for breakfast and she gives you
   two fried eggs and you eat
   both of them, who is better in arithmetic,
   you or your mother?

Carl Sandburg

Questions

Do trains get tired of running
And woodworms bored with holes
Are tunnels tired of darkness
And stones of being so old?

Do shadows tire of sunshine
Do tellys tire of fame
And footballs tire of kicking
And puddles tire of rain?

Does water tire of spilling
And fires of being too hot
And smells get tired of smelling
And chickenpox of spots?

I do not know the answers,
I'll ask them all one day . . .
But I get tired of working,
BUT NEVER TIRED OF PLAY.

Peter Dixon

Down by the School Gate

There goes the bell
it's half-past three
and down by the school gate
you will see . . .

. . . ten mums talk talk talking
nine babies squawk squawking
eight toddlers all squabbling
seven grans on bikes wobbling

six dogs bark bark barking
five cars stopping, parking
four child-minders running
three bus-drivers sunning

two teenagers dating
one lollipop man waiting . . .

The school is out,
it's half-past three
and the first to the school gate
. . . is me!

Wes Magee

Kept In

They tell me off —
but not one of them knows
what I could do
if I really chose.

I'm from further off than Mars,
the lad from way beyond the stars.
With a Ho and a Hoo
I could turn you all blue.

I wear the same shape.
You think I'm like you.
I keep very quiet
and watch what you do.

But I'm the one from far away,
don't think that I intend to stay.
With a flash and a crash
I could turn you to ash.

Don't keep me too long
I feel in my bones
something odd's going to happen,
Mr Schoolmaster Jones.

Barbara Giles

The Performing Bag

The plastic bag that once was full
Of coloured sweets was empty and lost
And lay against the playground wall,
Flat and still among the dust.

But a wind came up the road,
Brushing back the hair of the grass,
Trying to unbutton people's coats
And teasing the leaves as it passed.

It felt its way inside the bag
Like a hand inside a glove
And like a puppet waking up
The plastic bag began to move.

As the air inside it puffed it out,
The bag that was lying sad and flat
Began to waggle its corners about
And nodded its head this way and that.

It dodged its way between the children
Who watched it carried high in the sky
And disappear on the hand of the wind,
Waving them goodbye.

Stanley Cook

Flowering Umbrellas

Umbrellas are folded up like buds.
But umbrella buds don't open in the sun.
They flower in the rain instead
In all kinds of colours: black, green, and red,
Brown and white, and checked and striped.
Outside the school in the rain mothers stand
With umbrella flowers growing from their hands.

Stanley Cook

Road Up

What's wrong with the road?
Why all this hush? —
They've given an anaesthetic
In the lunch-hour rush.

They've shaved off the tarmac
With a pneumatic drill,
And bandaged the traffic
To a dead standstill.

Surgeons in shirt-sleeves
Bend over the patient,
Intent on a major
Operation.

Don't dare sneeze!
Don't dare shout!
The road is having
Its appendix out.

Norman Nicholson

Lost Rainbow

One day
coming home from school
(where else?)
I found a rainbow.
Lost
and sad
and torn
and broken
on a garage forecourt.
I picked it up,
wrapped it in a Wonderloaf wrapper
(which was also lost)
and took it home
where I warmed it
and dried it
in front of my mother's fire.
But it died.

I think it must have been
a very old rainbow.

Peter Dixon

The North Wind Doth Blow

The north wind doth blow
And we shall have snow,
And what will poor robin do then, poor thing?
 He'll sit in a barn,
 And keep himself warm,
And hide his head under his wing, poor thing!

The north wind doth blow
And we shall have snow,
And what will the dormouse do then, poor thing?
 Roll'd up like a ball,
 In his nest snug and small,
He'll sleep till warm weather comes in, poor thing!

The north wind doth blow
And we shall have snow,
And what will the children do then, poor things?
 When lessons are done,
 They must skip, jump, and run,
Until they have made themselves warm, poor things!

Anon

The North Wind

Once, when I was young I knew the wind.
I called 'Wi-ind, North Wi-ind'
And it came,
   tramping the grass so that it lay flat,
And whinnied high and shrill like a whistle.
I saddled it with imagination,
   and bridled it with dreams.

And I got on and we went, and the trees
   bowed down in our passing.
I was exhilarated with the speed
   and lay down on his neck to keep
   balance.
And his snowy mane whipped about my face.
His unshod hoofs made no sound
   as he trod on the stars.
His breath made icicles on the houses
   we passed
And then he bucked.

Joanne Lysyk

What is the Sun?

the Sun is an orange dinghy
  sailing across a calm sea

it is a gold coin
  dropped down a drain in heaven

the Sun is a yellow beach ball
  kicked high into the summer sky

it is a red thumb-print
  on a sheet of pale blue paper

the Sun is a milk bottle's golden top
  floating in a puddle

Wes Magee

The Echoing Green

The sun does arise,
And make happy the skies;
The merry bells ring
To welcome the spring;
The skylark and thrush,
The birds of the bush,
Sing louder around
To the bells' cheerful sound,
While our sports shall be seen
On the Echoing Green.

Old John, with white hair,
Does laugh away care,
Sitting under the oak,
Among the old folk.
They laugh at our play,
And soon they all say:
'Such, such were the joys
When we all, girls and boys,
In our youth-time were seen
On the Echoing Green.'

Till the little ones, weary,
No more can be merry;
The sun does descend,
And our sports have an end.
Round the laps of their mothers
Many sisters and brothers,
Like birds in their nest,
Are ready for rest,
And sport no more seen
On the darkening Green.

William Blake

Sunflakes

If sunlight fell like snowflakes,
gleaming yellow and so bright,
we could build a sunman,
we could have a sunball fight,
we could watch the sunflakes
drifting in the sky.
We could go sleighing
in the middle of July
through sundrifts and sunbanks,
we could ride a sunmobile,
and we could touch sunflakes —
I wonder how they'd feel.

Frank Asch

Cold Feet

They have all gone across
They are all turning to see
They are all shouting 'come on'
They are all waiting for me.

I look through the gaps in the footway
And my heart shrivels with fear,
For far below the river is flowing
So quick and so cold and so clear.

And all that there is between it
And me falling down there is this:
A few wooden planks — not very thick —
And between each, a little abyss.

The holes get right under my sandals.
I can see straight through to the rocks,
And if I don't look, I can feel it,
Just there, through my shoes and my socks.

Suppose my feet and my legs withered up
And slipped through the slats like a rug?
Suppose I suddenly went very thin
Like the baby that slid down the plug?

I know that it cannot happen
But suppose that it did, what then?
Would they be able to find me
And take me back home again?

They have all gone across
They are all waiting to see
They are all shouting 'come on' —
But they'll have to carry me.

Brian Lee

A Bridge

A bridge is a giant on hands and knees
Kneeling down to fill a gap
And let people cross it on his back.

A bridge is a giant of stone or steel
With a back so hard he doesn't feel
The prodding of sticks or hammering of heels.

A bridge is a giant who carries the road
And the lorries on it with heavy loads,
A giant who stays there night and day
And never gets up and goes away.

Stanley Cook

from 'The Cataract of Lodore'

The Cataract strong
Then plunges along,
Striking and raging
As if a war waging
Its caverns and rocks among:
Rising and leaping,
Sinking and creeping,
Swelling and sweeping,
Showering and springing,
Flying and flinging,
Writhing and ringing,
Eddying and whisking,
Spouting and frisking,
Turning and twisting,
Around and around
With endless rebound!
Smiting and fighting,
A sight to delight in;
Confounding, astounding,
Dizzying and deafening the ear with its sound.

Robert Southey

The Brook

I come from haunts of coot and tern,
  I make a sudden sally,
And sparkle out among the fern,
  To bicker down a valley.

By thirty hills I hurry down,
  Or slip between the ridges,
By twenty thorps, a little town,
  And half a hundred bridges.

Till last by Philip's farm I flow
  To join the brimming river,
For men may come and men may go,
  But I go on for ever.

I chatter over stony ways,
  In little sharps and trebles,
I bubble into eddying bays,
  I babble on the pebbles.

With many a curve my banks I fret
  By many a field and fallow,
And many a fairy foreland set
  With willow-weed and mallow.

I chatter, chatter, as I flow
  To join the brimming river,
For men may come and men may go,
  But I go on for ever.

I wind about, and in and out,
  With here a blossom sailing,
And here and there a lusty trout,
  And here and there a grayling,

And here and there a foamy flake
  Upon me, as I travel
With many a silvery waterbreak
  Above the golden gravel.

And draw them all along, and flow
  To join the brimming river,
For men may come and men may go,
  But I go on for ever.

I steal by lawns and grassy plots,
  I slide by hazel covers;
I move the sweet forget-me-nots
  That grow for happy lovers.

I slip, I slide, I gloom, I glance,
  Among my skimming swallows;
I make the netted sunbeam dance
  Against my sandy shallows.

I murmur under moon and stars
  In brambly wildernesses;
I linger by my shingly bars;
  I loiter round my cresses;

And out again I curve and flow
  To join the brimming river,
For men may come and men may go,
  But I go on for ever.

Alfred, Lord Tennyson

The Tale of the Estuary and the Hedge

'Come,' said the small slimy
estuary pleasantly,
'come!' to the hedge that guarded
the door of the low-lying meadow.

'Follow me along my easy
course,' smiled the mud. 'Oh
your butter won't turn,
your daisies won't run!
I assure you, you won't be away for long.'

Doubtful, the hedge packed
its hawthorn blooms, sparrow nests
and ditchweeds neatly in a bundle,
to follow — with a guilty look behind:
Had the meadow noticed?

Hour on hour lazily
the little estuary
crept and curved,
the hedge trotting after.

The air became brighter,
new the birds that swam
or perched momentarily,
net-heaps ousting ploughs
and the estuary gaining in girth.

Now, like an ambush
round the corner, the land
stops! The hedge is lost!

'It is The Sea — it is only
the sea,' smiles on the estuary.
'Don't be yellow-hearted! Come,
follow,
    I'll
      be
        leading
      you . . .'

Libby Houston

Grim and Gloomy

Oh, grim and gloomy,
So grim and gloomy
Are the caves beneath the sea.
Oh, rare but roomy
And bare and boomy,
Those salt sea caverns be.

Oh, slim and slimy
Or grey and grimy
Are the animals of the sea.
Salt and oozy
And safe and snoozy
The caves where those animals be.

Hark to the shuffling,
Huge and snuffling,
Ravenous, cavernous, great sea-beasts!
But fair and fabulous,
Tintinnabulous,
Gay and fabulous are their feasts.

Ah, but the queen of the sea,
The querulous, perilous sea!
How the curls of her tresses
The pearls on her dresses,
Sway and swirl in the waves,
How cosy and dozy,
How sweet ring-a-rosy
Her bower in the deep-sea caves!

Oh, rare but roomy
And bare and boomy
Those caverns under the sea,
And grave and grandiose,
Safe and sandiose
The dens of her denizens be.

James Reeves

Sea Fever

I must down to the seas again, to the lonely sea and the sky,
And all I ask is a tall ship and a star to steer her by,
And the wheel's kick and the wind's song and the white sail's shaking,
And a grey mist on the sea's face and a grey dawn breaking.

I must down to the seas again, for the call of the running tide
Is a wild call and a clear call that may not be denied;
And all I ask is a windy day with the white clouds flying,
And the flung spray and the blown spume, and the seagulls crying.

I must down to the seas again, to the vagrant gypsy life,
To the gull's way and the whale's way where the wind's like a
    whetted knife;
And all I ask is a merry yarn from a laughing fellow-rover,
And quiet sleep and a sweet dream when the long trick's over.

John Masefield

The Jumblies

They went to sea in a Sieve, they did,
   In a Sieve they went to sea:
In spite of all their friends could say,
On a winter's morn, on a stormy day,
   In a Sieve they went to sea!
And when the Sieve turned round and round,
And everyone cried, 'You'll all be drowned!'
They called aloud, 'Our Sieve ain't big,
But we don't care a button! we don't care a fig!
   In a Sieve we'll go to sea!'
     Far and few, far and few,
       Are the lands where the Jumblies live;
      Their heads are green, and their hands are blue,
       And they went to sea in a Sieve.

They sailed away in a Sieve, they did,
   In a Sieve they sailed so fast,
With only a beautiful pea-green veil
Tied with a riband by way of a sail,
   To a small tobacco-pipe mast;
And everyone said, who saw them go,
'O won't they be soon upset, you know!
For the sky is dark, and the voyage is long,
And happen what may, it's extremely wrong
   In a Sieve to sail so fast!'
      Far and few, far and few,
         Are the lands where the Jumblies live;
         Their heads are green, and their hands are blue,
            And they went to sea in a Sieve.

The water it soon came in, it did,
    The water it soon came in;
So to keep them dry, they wrapped their feet
In a pinky paper all folded neat,
    And they fastened it down with a pin.
And they passed the night in a crockery-jar,
And each of them said, 'How wise we are!
Though the sky be dark, and the voyage be long,
Yet we never can think we were rash or wrong,
    While round in our Sieve we spin!'
    Far and few, far and few,
        Are the lands where the Jumblies live;
        Their heads are green, and their hands are blue,
        And they went to sea in a Sieve.

And all night long they sailed away;
    And when the sun went down,
They whistled and warbled a moony song
To the echoing sound of a coppery gong,
    In the shade of the mountains brown.
'O Timballoo! How happy we are,
When we live in a sieve and a crockery-jar,
And all night long in the moonlight pale,
We sail away with a pea-green sail,
    In the shade of the mountains brown!'
        Far and few, far and few,
            Are the lands where the Jumblies live;
            Their heads are green, and their hands are blue,
            And they went to sea in a Sieve.

They sailed to the Western Sea, they did,
    To a land all covered with trees,
And they bought an Owl, and a useful Cart,
And a pound of Rice, and a Cranberry Tart,
    And a hive of silvery Bees.
And they bought a Pig, and some green Jackdaws,
And a lovely Monkey with lollipop paws,
And forty bottles of Ring-Bo-Ree,
    And no end of Stilton Cheese.
        Far and few, far and few,
            Are the lands where the Jumblies live;
            Their heads are green, and their hands are blue,
            And they went to sea in a Sieve.

And in twenty years they all came back,
    In twenty years or more,
And everyone said, 'How tall they've grown!
For they've been to the Lakes, and the Torrible Zone,
    And the hills of the Chankly Bore';
And they drank their health, and gave them a feast
Of dumplings made of beautiful yeast;
And everyone said, 'If we only live,
We too will go to sea in a Sieve,
    To the hills of the Chankly Bore!'
        Far and few, far and few,
            Are the lands where the Jumblies live;
            Their heads are green, and their hands are blue,
                And they went to sea in a Sieve.

Edward Lear

Once the Wind

Once the wind
said to the sea
I am sad
      And the sea said
Why
      And the wind said
Because I
am not blue like the sky
or like you

      So the sea said what's
so sad about that
         Lots
of things are blue
or red or other colours too
     but nothing
neither sea nor sky
can blow so strong
or sing so long as you

     And the sea looked sad
      So the wind said
Why

Shake Keane

Stones by the Sea

Smooth and flat, grey, brown and white,
Winter and summer, noon and night,
Tumbling together for a thousand ages,
We ought to be wiser than Eastern sages.
But no doubt we stones are foolish as most,
So we don't say much on our stretch of coast.
Quiet and peaceful we mainly sit,
And when storms come up we grumble a bit.

James Reeves

The Sea

The sea is a hungry dog,
Giant and grey.
He rolls on the beach all day.
With his clashing teeth and shaggy jaws
Hour upon hour he gnaws
The rumbling, tumbling stones,
And 'Bones, bones, bones, bones!'
The giant sea-dog moans,
Licking his greasy paws.

And when the night wind roars
And the moon rocks in the stormy cloud,
He bounds to his feet and snuffs and sniffs,
Shaking his wet sides over the cliffs,
And howls and hollos long and loud.

But on quiet days in May or June,
When even the grasses on the dune
Play no more their reedy tune,
With his head between his paws
He lies on the sandy shores,
So quiet, so quiet, he scarcely snores.

James Reeves

The Sea's Treasures

In swept the sea
With a swirl and a swish,
It shimmered and whispered,
'Choose what you wish.'

And the sea showed its treasures
At the edge of the shore,
Shining bright pebbles
And shells by the score.

Long ribbons of seaweed
That shone gold and red,
'I'll share them, I'll share,'
The sea softly said.

Daphne Lister

Cargoes

Quinquereme of Nineveh from distant Ophir
Rowing home to haven in sunny Palestine,
With a cargo of ivory,
And apes and peacocks,
Sandalwood, cedarwood, and sweet white wine.

Stately Spanish galleon coming from the Isthmus,
Dipping through the Tropics by the palm-green shores,
With a cargo of diamonds,
Emeralds, amethysts,
Topazes, and cinnamon, and gold moidores.

Dirty British coaster with a salt-caked smoke stack
Butting through the Channel in the mad March days,
With a cargo of Tyne coal,
Road-rail, pig-lead,
Firewood, iron-ware, and cheap tin trays.

John Masefield

The Sands of Dee

'O Mary, go and call the cattle home,
    And call the cattle home,
    And call the cattle home,
  Across the sands of Dee!'
The western wind was wild and dank with foam,
  And all alone went she.

The western tide crept up along the sand,
    And o'er and o'er the sand,
    And round and round the sand,
  As far as eye could see.
The rolling mist came down and hid the land:
  And never home came she.

'Oh! is it weed, or fish, or floating hair —
    A tress of golden hair,
    A drowned maiden's hair,
  Above the nets at sea?
Was never salmon yet that shone so fair
  Among the stakes on Dee.'

They rowed her in across the rolling foam,
    The cruel crawling foam,
    The cruel hungry foam,
  To her grave beside the sea:
But still the boatmen hear her call the cattle home
  Across the sands of Dee.

Charles Kingsley

Daughter of the Sea

bog seeper
moss creeper
growing restless
getting steeper

trickle husher
swish and rusher
stone leaper
splash and gusher

foam flicker
mirror slicker
pebble pusher
boulder kicker

still pool
don't be fooled
shadow tricker
keeping cool

leap lunger
crash plunger
free fall
with thunder under

idle winder
youth behind her
little wonder
daily grinder

garbage binner
dump it in her
never mind her
dog's dinner

plastic bagger
old lagger
oil skinner
wharf nagger

cargo porter
weary water
tide dragger
long lost daughter

of the sea
the sea the sea
has caught her
up in its arms and set her free

Philip Gross

A Green Prayer

Save me a clean stream, flowing
to unpolluted seas;

lend me the bare earth, growing
untamed flowers and trees.

May I share safe skies
when I wake, every day,

with birds and butterflies?
Grant me a space where I can play

with water, rocks, trees, and sand;
lend me forests, rivers, hills, and sea.

Keep me a place in this old land,
somewhere to grow, somewhere to be.

Jane Whittle

In Beauty May I Walk

In beauty	may I walk
All day long	may I walk
Through the returning seasons	may I walk
Beautifully will I possess again	
Beautifully birds	
Beautifully joyful birds	
On the trail marked with pollen	may I walk
With grasshoppers about my feet	may I walk
With dew about my feet	may I walk
With beauty	may I walk
With beauty before me	may I walk
With beauty behind me	may I walk
With beauty above me	may I walk
With beauty all around me	may I walk
In old age, wandering on a trail of beauty, lively,	may I walk
In old age, wandering on a trail of beauty, living again,	may I walk
It is finished in beauty	
It is finished in beauty	

Navajo

Spells

I dance and dance without any feet —
This is the spell of the ripening wheat.

With never a tongue I've a tale to tell —
This is the meadow-grasses' spell.

I give you health without any fee —
This is the spell of the apple-tree.

I rhyme and riddle without any book —
This is the spell of the bubbling brook.

Without any legs I run for ever —
This is the spell of the mighty river.

I fall for ever and not at all —
This is the spell of the waterfall.

Without a voice I roar aloud —
This is the spell of the thunder-cloud.

No button or seam has my white coat —
This is the spell of the leaping goat.

I can cheat strangers with never a word —
This is the spell of the cuckoo-bird.

We have tongues in plenty but speak no names —
This is the spell of the fiery flames.

The creaking door has a spell to riddle —
I play a tune without any fiddle.

James Reeves

Trees are Great

Trees are great, they just stand and wait
They don't cry when they're teased
They don't eat much and they seldom shout
Trees are easily pleased

Trees are great, they like to congregate
For meetings in the park
They dance and sway, they stay all day
And talk till well after dark

Trees are great, they accept their fate
When it's pouring down with rain
They don't wear macs, it runs off their backs
But you never hear them complain

So answer me, please, if there weren't any trees
Where would naughty boys climb?
Where would lovers carve their names?
Where would little birds nest?
Where would we hang the leaves?

Roger McGough

I Meant to do My Work Today

I meant to do my work today —
But a brown bird sang in the apple tree,
And a butterfly flitted across the field,
And all the leaves were calling me.

And the wind went sighing over the land,
Tossing the grasses to and fro,
And a rainbow held out its shining hand —
So what could I do but laugh and go?

Richard le Gallienne

Loveliest of Trees

Loveliest of trees, the cherry now
Is hung with bloom along the bough,
And stands about the woodland ride
Wearing white for Eastertide.

Now, of my threescore years and ten,
Twenty will not come again,
And take from seventy springs a score,
It only leaves me fifty more.

And since to look at things in bloom
Fifty springs are little room,
About the woodlands I will go
To see the cherry hung with snow.

A. E. Housman

Leaves in the Yard

Leaves have the lightest footfall
Of all who come in the yard.
They play rounders, they play tig,
They play no-holds-barred.

Late, when people are all asleep
Still they scamper and weave.
They play robbers, they play cops,
They play Adam-and-Eve.

Tap, tap, on the pavement,
Flit, flit, in the air:
The sentry-going bat wonders what they're at,
The blank back-windows stare.

When they rest, the wind rests;
When they go, he goes too;
They play tiptoe, they play mouse,
He shouts *hoo*.

Summer, they fidgeted on trees,
Then autumn called 'Enough!'
They play leapfrog, they play fights,
They play blind-man's-buff.

Ragged, swept in corners,
Fallen beyond recall,
Ragged and old, soon to be mould, —
But light of heart wins all.

Hal Summers

The Way through the Woods

They shut the road through the woods
  Seventy years ago.
Weather and rain have undone it again,
  And now you would never know
There was once a road through the woods
  Before they planted the trees.

It is underneath the coppice and heath,
  And the thin anemones.
  Only the keeper sees
That, where the ring-dove broods,
  And the badgers roll at ease,
There was once a road through the woods.

Yet, if you enter the woods
  Of a summer evening late,
When the night-air cools on the trout-ringed pools
  Where the otter whistles his mate,
(They fear not men in the woods,
  Because they see so few)
You will hear the beat of a horse's feet
  And the swish of a skirt in the dew,
  Steadily cantering through
The misty solitudes,
  As though they perfectly knew
The old lost road through the woods . . .
But there is no road through the woods.

Rudyard Kipling

My Heart's in the Highlands

My heart's in the Highlands, my heart is not here;
My heart's in the Highlands a-chasing the deer;
Chasing the wild deer, and following the roe,
My heart's in the Highlands, wherever I go.
Farewell to the Highlands, farewell to the North,
The birth-place of valour, the country of worth;
Wherever I wander, wherever I rove,
The hills of the Highlands for ever I love.

Farewell to the mountains, high cover'd with snow;
Farewell to the straths and green valleys below;
Farewell to the forests and wild-hanging woods;
Farewell to the torrents and loud-pouring floods.
My heart's in the Highlands, my heart is not here;
My heart's in the Highlands a-chasing the deer;
Chasing the wild deer, and following the roe,
My heart's in the Highlands, wherever I go.

Robert Burns

To a Squirrel at Kyle-Na-No

Come play with me.
Why should you run
Through the shaking tree
As though I'd a gun
To strike you dead?
When all I would do
Is to scratch your head
And let you go.

W. B. Yeats

What in the World?

What in the world
goes whiskery friskery
meowling and prowling
napping and lapping
at silky milk?

Psst,
What is it?

What in the world
goes leaping and beeping
onto a lily pad onto a log
onto a tree stump or down to the bog?

Splash, blurp,
Kerchurp!

What in the world
goes gnawing and pawing
scratching and latching
sniffing and squiffing
nibbling for tidbits of left-over cheese?
Please?

What in the world
jumps with a hop and a bump
and a tail that can thump
has pink pointy ears and a twitchy nose
looking for anything crunchy that grows?
A carroty lettucey cabbagey luncheon
To munch on?

What in the world
climbs chattering pattering swinging from trees
like a flying trapeze
with a tail that can curl
like the rope the cowboys twirl?
Wahoo!
Here's a banana for you!

What in the world
goes stalking and balking
running and sunning
thumping and dumping
lugging and hugging
swinging and singing
wriggling and giggling
sliding and hiding
throwing and knowing and
growing and growing
much too big for
last year's clothes?
Who knows?

Eve Merriam

Hlep

Something has gone wrog in the garden.
There are doffadils blooming in the nose-beds,
And all over the griss dandeloons
Wave their ridigulous powdered wigs.

Under the wipping willop, in the pond
Where the whiter-lollies flute,
I see goldfinches swamming
And the toepaddles changing into fargs.

The griss itself is an unusual shade of groon
And the gote has come loose from its honges.
It's all extrepely worlying!
Helg me, some baddy! Heap me!

And it's not unly in the ganden.
These trumbles have fellowed me indares.
The toble has grown an extra log
And the Tally won't get Baby-See-Too.

Even my trusty Tygerwriter
Is producing the most peaqueueliar worms.
Helg me Sam Biddy. Kelp me!
Helg! HOLP! HELLO!!

Gerard Benson

Mumbling Bees

All around the garden flowers
Big velvet bees are bumbling,
They hover low and as they go
They're mumbling, mumbling, mumbling.

To lavender and snapdragons
The busy bees keep coming,
And all the busy afternoon
They're humming, humming, humming.

Inside each bell-shaped flower and rose
They busily go stumbling,
Collecting pollen all day long
And bumbling, bumbling, bumbling.

Daphne Lister

Wasps

Wasps in brightly
Coloured vests,
Chewing wood,
To make their nests.

Wasps, like rockets,
Zooming high,
Then dropping down
Where peaches lie.

Anne Ruddick

115

The Common Cormorant

The common cormorant or shag
Lays eggs inside a paper bag
The reason you will see no doubt
It is to keep the lightning out.
But what these unobservant birds
Have never noticed is that herds
Of wandering bears may come with buns
And steal the bags to hold the crumbs.

Anon

The Hen and the Carp

  Once, in a roostery
there lived a speckled hen, and whenever she laid an egg this hen
  ecstatically cried:
'O progeny miraculous, particular spectaculous,
  what a wonderful hen am I!'

  Down in a pond nearby
perchance a fat and broody carp
was basking, but her ears were sharp —
  she heard Dame Cackle cry:
'O progeny miraculous, particular spectaculous,
  what a wonderful hen am I!'

  'Ah, Cackle,' bubbled she,
'for your single egg, O silly one,
I lay at least a million;
  suppose for each I cried:
"O progeny miraculous, particular spectaculous!"
  what a hullaballoo there'd be!'

Ian Serraillier

a black dot

a black dot
a jelly tot

a scum-nail
a jiggle-tail

a leg-kicker
a sitting slicker

a panting puffer
a fly-snuffer

a high hopper
a belly-flopper

a catalogue
  to make me

   FROG

Libby Houston

118

Miss! Sue is Kissing

Miss! Sue is kissing
the tadpoles again.
She is, Miss. I did,
I asked her. She said
something about catching
him young. Getting one
her own age. I don't know,
Miss. She keeps whispering
'Prince, Prince.' Isn't that
a dog's name, Miss?

Michael Richards

The Little Turtle

There was a little turtle.
He lived in a box.
He swam in a puddle.
He climbed on the rocks.

He snapped at a mosquito.
He snapped at a flea.
He snapped at a minnow.
And he snapped at me.

He caught the mosquito.
He caught the flea.
He caught the minnow.
But he didn't catch me.

Vachel Lindsay

119

About the Teeth of Sharks

The thing about a shark is — teeth,
One row above, one row beneath.

Now take a close look. Do you find
It has another row behind?

Still closer — here, I'll hold your hat:
Has it a third row behind that?

Now look in and . . . Look out! Oh my,
I'll *never* know now! Well, goodbye.

John Ciardi

Infant Innocence

The Grizzly Bear is huge and wild;
He has devoured the infant child.
The infant child is not aware
He has been eaten by the bear.

A. E. Housman

How Doth the Little Crocodile

How doth the little crocodile
    Improve his shining tail;
And pour the waters of the Nile
    On every golden scale!

How cheerfully he seems to grin,
    How neatly spreads his claws,
And welcomes little fishes in,
    With gently smiling jaws!

Lewis Carroll

The Considerate Crocodile

There was once a considerate crocodile
Who lay on the banks of the river Nile
And he swallowed a fish with a face of woe,
While his tears ran fast to the stream below.
'I am mourning,' said he, 'the untimely fate
Of the dear little fish that I just now ate!'

Amos R. Wells

Three Birds

Three birds flew in a clouded sky.
One was you and one was I
   And no one knows the other.

The sky was heavy, soft and warm,
And off we flew to cheat the storm,
   You, I, and the other.

To cheat the storm, away we flew;
One was white and one was blue.
   A raven was the other.

We flew to far-off countries, where
Soft waters speak to brittle air,
   Always with the other.

And there we bathed in silver springs
And shook the water from our wings;
   And with us came the other.

And in those fair, enchanted lands,
We built our nest upon the sands;
   And still with us the other.

And when we sang, the trilling notes
Like liquid, rippled from our throats;
   He never sang, that other.

Three birds mount toward the sun;
One is you, and I am one
   And no one knows the other.

Gerard Benson

Roger the Dog

Asleep he wheezes at his ease.
He only wakes to scratch his fleas.

He hogs the fire, he bakes his head
As if it were a loaf of bread.

He's just a sack of snoring dog.
You can lug him like a log.

You can roll him with your foot,
He'll stay snoring where he's put.

I take him out for exercise,
He rolls in cowclap up to his eyes.

He will not race, he will not romp,
He saves his strength for gobble and chomp.

He'll work as hard as you could wish
Emptying his dinner dish,

Then flops flat, and digs down deep,
Like a miner, into sleep.

Ted Hughes

Cat in the Dark

Look at that!
Look at that!

But when you look
there's no cat.

Without a purr
just a flash of fur
and gone
like a ghost.

The most
you see
are two tiny
green traffic lights
staring at the night.

John Agard

The Cat and the Moon

The cat went here and there
And the moon spun round like a top,
And the nearest kin of the moon,
The creeping cat, looked up.
Black Minnaloushe stared at the moon,
For, wander and wail as he would,
The pure cold light in the sky
Troubled his animal blood.
Minnaloushe runs in the grass
Lifting his delicate feet.
Do you dance, Minnaloushe, do you dance?
When two close kindred meet,
What better than call a dance?
Maybe the moon may learn,
Tired of that courtly fashion,
A new dance turn.
Minnaloushe creeps through the grass
From moonlit place to place,
The sacred moon overhead
Has taken a new phase.
Does Minnaloushe know that his pupils
Will pass from change to change,
And that from round to crescent,
From crescent to round they range?
Minnaloushe creeps through the grass
Alone, important and wise,
And lifts to the changing moon
His changing eyes.

W. B. Yeats

Silver

Slowly, silently, now the moon
Walks the night in her silver shoon;
This way, and that, she peers, and sees
Silver fruit upon silver trees;
One by one the casements catch
Her beams beneath the silvery thatch;
Couched in his kennel, like a log,
With paws of silver sleeps the dog;
From their shadowy cote the white breasts peep
Of doves in a silver-feathered sleep;
A harvest mouse goes scampering by,
With silver claws, and silver eye;
And moveless fish in the water gleam,
By silver reeds in a silver stream.

Walter de la Mare

A Path to the Moon

From my front door there's a path to the moon
that nobody seems to see
tho it's marked with stones & grass & trees
there's nobody sees it but me.

You walk straight ahead for ten trees or so
turn left at the robin's song
follow the sound of the west wind down
past where the deer drink from the pond.

You take a right turn as the river bends
then where the clouds touch the earth
close your left eye & count up to ten
while twirling for all that you're worth.

And if you keep walking right straight ahead
clambering over the clouds
saying your mother's & father's names
over & over out loud

you'll come to the place where moonlight's born
the place where the moonbeams hide
and visit all of the crater sites
on the dark moon's secret side.

From my front door there's a path to the moon
that nobody seems to see
tho it's marked with stones & grass & trees
no one sees it but you & me.

B. P. Nichol

The Dark

I don't like the dark coming down on my head
It feels like a blanket thrown over the bed
I don't like the dark coming down on my head

I don't like the dark coming down over me
It feels like the room's full of things I can't see
I don't like the dark coming down over me

There isn't enough light from under the door
It only just reaches the edge of the floor
There isn't enough light from under the door

I wish that my dad hadn't put out the light
It feels like there's something that's just out of sight
I wish that my dad hadn't put out the light

But under the bedclothes it's warm and secure
You can't see the ceiling you can't see the floor
Yes, under the bedclothes it's warm and secure
So I think I'll stay here till it's daylight once more.

Adrian Henri

The Dark House

In a dark, dark wood, there was a dark, dark house,
And in that dark, dark house, there was a dark, dark room,
And in that dark, dark room, there was a dark, dark cupboard,
And in that dark, dark cupboard, there was a dark, dark shelf,
And in that dark, dark shelf, there was a dark, dark box,
And in that dark, dark box, there was a GHOST!

Anon

A Smuggler's Song

If you wake at midnight, and hear a horse's feet,
Don't go drawing back the blind, or looking in the street.
Them that asks no questions isn't told a lie.
Watch the wall, my darling, while the Gentlemen go by!
    Five and twenty ponies,
    Trotting through the dark —
    Brandy for the Parson,
    'Baccy for the Clerk;
    Laces for a lady, letters for a spy,
And watch the wall, my darling, while the Gentlemen go by!

Running round the woodlump if you chance to find
Little barrels, roped and tarred, all full of brandy-wine,
Don't you shout to come and look, nor use 'em for your play.
Put the brushwood back again — and they'll be gone next day!

If you see a stable-door setting open wide;
If you see a tired horse lying down inside;
If your mother mends a coat cut about and tore;
If the lining's wet and warm — don't you ask no more!

If you meet King George's men, dressed in blue and red,
You be careful what you say, and mindful what is said.
If they call you 'pretty maid', and chuck you 'neath the chin,
Don't you tell where no one is, nor yet where no one's been!

Knocks and footsteps round the house — whistles after dark —
You've no call for running out till the house-dogs bark.
Trusty's here, and *Pincher*'s here, and see how dumb they lie —
They don't fret to follow when the Gentlemen go by!

If you do as you've been told, 'likely there's a chance,
You'll be given a dainty doll, all the way from France,
With a cap of Valenciennes, and a velvet hood —
A present from the Gentlemen, along o' being good!
    Five and twenty ponies,
    Trotting through the dark —
    Brandy for the Parson,
    'Baccy for the Clerk.
Them that asks no questions isn't told a lie —
Watch the wall, my darling, while the Gentlemen go by!

Rudyard Kipling

The Night Mail

This is the night mail crossing the border,
Bringing the cheque and the postal order,
Letters for the rich, letters for the poor,
The shop at the corner and the girl next door,
Pulling up Beattock, a steady climb —
The gradient's against her but she's on time.

Past cotton grass and moorland boulder,
Shovelling white steam over her shoulder,
Snorting noisily as she passes
Silent miles of wind-bent grasses;
Birds turn their heads as she approaches,
Stare from the bushes at her blank-faced coaches;
Sheepdogs cannot turn her course,
They slumber on with paws across;
In the farm she passes no one wakes
But a jug in a bedroom gently shakes.

Dawn freshens, the climb is done.
Down towards Glasgow she descends
Towards the steam tugs, yelping down the glade of cranes
Towards the fields of apparatus, the furnaces
Set on the dark plain like gigantic chessmen.
All Scotland waits for her;
In the dark glens, beside the pale-green sea lochs,
Men long for news.

Letters of thanks, letters from banks,
Letters of joy from the girl and boy,
Receipted bills and invitations
To inspect new stock or visit relations,
And applications for situations,
And timid lovers' declarations,
And gossip, gossip from all the nations,
News circumstantial, news financial,
Letters with holiday snaps to enlarge in,
Letters with faces scrawled on the margin.
Letters from uncles, cousins, and aunts,
Letters to Scotland from the South of France,
Letters of condolence to Highlands and Lowlands,
Notes from overseas to the Hebrides;
Written on paper of every hue,
The pink, the violet, the white, and the blue,
The chatty, the catty, the boring, adoring,
The cold and official and the heart's outpouring,
Clever, stupid, short, and long,
The typed and the printed and the spelt all wrong.

Thousands are still asleep
Dreaming of terrifying monsters
Or a friendly tea beside the band at Cranston's or
     Crawford's;
Asleep in working Glasgow, asleep in well-set
     Edinburgh,
Asleep in granite Aberdeen.
They continue their dreams
But shall wake soon and long for letters.
And none will hear the postman's knock
Without a quickening of the heart,
For who can bear to feel himself forgotten?

W. H. Auden

The Ride-by-Nights

Up on their brooms the Witches stream,
Crooked and black in the crescent's gleam;
One foot high, and one foot low,
Bearded, cloaked, and cowled, they go.
'Neath Charlie's Wain they twitter and tweet,
And away they swarm 'neath the Dragon's feet.
With a whoop and a flutter they swing and sway,
And surge pell-mell down the Milky Way.
Betwixt the legs of the glittering Chair
They hover and squeak in the empty air.
Then round they swoop past the glimmering Lion
To where Sirius barks behind huge Orion;
Up, then, and over to wheel amain,
Under the silver, and home again.

Walter de la Mare

The Visitor

A crumbling churchyard, the sea and the moon;
The waves had gouged out grave and bone;
A man was walking, late and alone . . .

He saw a skeleton white on the ground,
A ring on a bony hand he found.

He ran home to his wife and gave her the ring.
'Oh, where did you get it?' He said not a thing.

'It's the prettiest ring in the world,' she said,
As it glowed on her finger. They skipped off to bed.

At midnight they woke. In the dark outside,
'Give me my ring!' a chill voice cried.

'What was that, William? What did it say?'
'Don't worry, my dear. It'll soon go away.'

'I'm coming!' A skeleton opened the door.
'Give me my ring!' It was crossing the floor.

'What was that, William? What did it say?'
'Don't worry, my dear. It'll soon go away.'

'I'm touching you now! I'm climbing the bed.'
The wife pulled the sheet right over her head.

It was torn from her grasp and tossed in the air:
'I'll drag you out of your bed by the hair!'

'What was that, William? What did it say?'
'Throw the ring through the window! THROW IT AWAY!'

She threw it. The skeleton leapt from the sill,
Scooped up the ring and clattered downhill,
Fainter . . . and fainter . . . Then all was still.

Ian Serraillier

Ghost in the Garden

The ghost in the garden
Cracks twigs as she treads
Shuffles the leaves
But isn't there

The ghost in the garden
Snaps back the brambles
So they spring against my legs
But isn't there

Draws spiders' webs across my face
Breathes mist on my cheek
Whispers with bird-breath down my ear
But isn't there

Tosses raindrops down from branches
Splashes the pond
Traces a face in it
That isn't mine

Moves shadows underneath the trees
Too tall, too thin, too tiny to be me

Spreads bindweed out to catch me
Flutters wild wings about my head
Tugs at my hair
But isn't there

And when I look
There's only the bend of grass
Where her running feet
Have smudged the dew

And there's only the sigh
Of her laughter
Trickling
Like
Moonlight
On
Wet
Weeds.

Berlie Doherty

House Ghosts

Airing cupboard ghosts
hold music practices
inside the water tank.

Television ghosts
poke crooked fingers
across your favourite programme.

Chimney ghosts
sing one-note songs
over and over in owly voices.

Vacuum-cleaner ghosts
roar and the dust obeys them,
into the bag.

But the worst ghost
hides under your bed at night.

He makes no noise at all.

Irene Rawnsley

Mr Nobody

I know a funny little man,
  As quiet as a mouse,
Who does the mischief that is done
  In everybody's house!
There's no one ever sees his face,
  And yet we all agree
That every plate we break was cracked
  By Mr Nobody.

'Tis he who always tears our books,
  Who leaves the door ajar,
He pulls the buttons from our shirts,
  And scatters pins afar;
That squeaking door will always squeak
  For, prithee, don't you see,
We leave the oiling to be done
  By Mr Nobody.

He puts damp wood upon the fire,
  That kettles cannot boil;
His are the feet that bring in mud,
  And all the carpets soil.
The papers always are mislaid,
  Who had them last but he?
There's not one tosses them about
  But Mr Nobody.

The finger-marks upon the door
  By none of us are made;
We never leave the blinds unclosed,
  To let the curtains fade;
The ink we never spill; the boots
  That lying round you see
Are not our boots; they all belong
  To Mr Nobody.

Anon

Talk About Caves

Talk about caves! Tell us,
tell us about them!
What's a cave, what's it like?

'My strongroom, mine,' said the Dragon,
'where I hid my gorgeous gold!'
But he lay gloating there so long,
in the end he turned to stone —
crawl down his twisting throat, you can,
for his breath's quite cold.

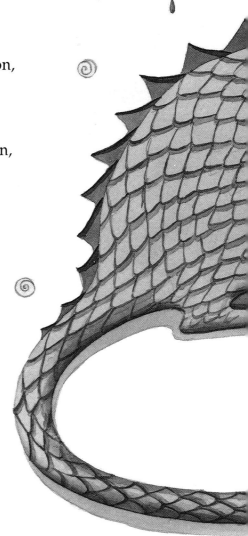

'My house once,'
whispered the Caveman's ghost.
'O it was good
wrapped in fur by the fire to hear
the roaring beasts in the wood
and sleep sound in earth's arms!
(If you find my old knife there,
you can keep it.)'

'My bolthole from the beginning,'
Night said,
'where I've stayed
safe from my enemy, Day.
I watch through a crack the sun
beating away at the door —
"Open up!" he shouts.
He'll never get in!'

'My home, always,' said Water.
'I wash my hands here
and slow as I like I make
new beds to lie on
in secret rooms
with pillows and curtains
and lovely ornaments,
pillars and plumes,
statues and thrones —
what colours the dark hides!
I shape earth's bones.'

'Don't disturb me,' the Bat said.
'This is where I hang my weary head.'

Libby Houston

Three Wise Old Women

Three wise old women were they, were they,
Who went to walk on a winter day:
One carried a basket to hold some berries,
One carried a ladder to climb for cherries,
The third, and she was the wisest one,
Carried a fan to keep off the sun.

But they went so far, and they went so fast,
They quite forgot their way at last,
So one of the wise women cried in a fright,
'Suppose we should meet a bear tonight!
Suppose he should eat me!' 'And me!!' 'And me!!!'
'What is to be done?' cried all the three.

'Dear, dear!' said one, 'we'll climb a tree,
There out of the way of the bears we'll be.'
But there wasn't a tree for miles around;
They were too frightened to stay on the ground,
So they climbed their ladder up to the top,
And sat there screaming 'We'll drop! We'll drop!

But the wind was strong as wind could be,
And blew their ladder right out to sea;
So the three wise women were all afloat
In a leaky ladder instead of a boat,
And every time the waves rolled in,
Of course the poor things were wet to the skin.

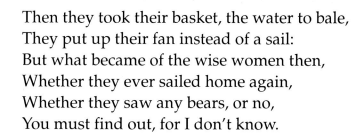

Then they took their basket, the water to bale,
They put up their fan instead of a sail:
But what became of the wise women then,
Whether they ever sailed home again,
Whether they saw any bears, or no,
You must find out, for I don't know.

Elizabeth T. Corbett

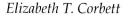

The Riddling Knight

There were three sisters fair and bright,
  Jennifer, Gentle, and Rosemary,
And they three loved one valiant knight —
  As the dow flies over the mulberry-tree.

The eldest sister let him in,
And barr'd the door with a silver pin.

The second sister made his bed,
And placed soft pillows under his head.

The youngest sister that same night
Was resolved for to wed wi' this valiant knight.

'And if you can answer questions three,
O then, fair maid, I'll marry wi' thee.

'O what is louder nor a horn,
Or what is sharper nor a thorn?

'Or what is heavier nor the lead,
Or what is better nor the bread?

'Or what is longer nor the way,
Or what is deeper nor the sea?' —

'O shame is louder nor a horn,
And hunger is sharper nor a thorn.

'O sin is heavier nor the lead,
The blessing's better nor the bread.

'O the wind is longer nor the way
And love is deeper nor the sea.'

'You have answer'd aright my questions three,'
  Jennifer, Gentle, and Rosemary;
'And now, fair maid, I'll marry wi' thee,'
  As the dow flies over the mulberry-tree.

Anon

149

The Dong with a Luminous Nose

When awful darkness and silence reign
Over the great Gromboolian plain,
Through the long, long wintry nights;
When the angry breakers roar
As they beat on the rocky shore;
When the Storm-clouds brood on the towering heights
Of the Hills of the Chankly Bore:

Then, through the vast and gloomy dark,
There moves what seems a fiery spark,
A lonely spark with silvery rays
Piercing the coal-black night,
A Meteor strange and bright:
Hither and thither the vision strays,
A single lurid light.

Slowly it wanders, pauses, creeps,
Anon it sparkles, flashes, and leaps;
And ever as onward it gleaming goes
A light on the Bong-tree stems it throws.
And those who watch at that midnight hour
From Hall or Terrace, or lofty Tower,
Cry, as the wild light passes along,
'The Dong! the Dong!
The wandering Dong through the forest goes!
The Dong! the Dong!
The Dong with a luminous Nose!'

Long years ago
The Dong was happy and gay,
Till he fell in love with a Jumbly Girl
Who came to those shores one day,
For the Jumblies came in a sieve, they did,
Landing at eve near the Zemmery Fidd
Where the Oblong Oysters grow,
And the rocks are smooth and grey.
And all the woods and the valleys rang
With the Chorus they daily and nightly sang —

'Far and few, far and few,
Are the lands where the Jumblies live;
Their heads are green, and their hands are blue
And they went to sea in a sieve.'

Happily, happily passed those days!
While the cheerful Jumblies stayed;
They danced in circlets all night long,
To the plaintive pipe of the lively Dong,
In moonlight, shine, or shade.
For day and night he was always there
By the side of the Jumbly Girl so fair,
With her sky-blue hands, and her sea-green hair.
Till the morning came of that hateful day
When the Jumblies sailed in their sieve away,
And the Dong was left on the cruel shore
Gazing-gazing for evermore,
Ever keeping his weary eyes on
That pea-green sail on the far horizon,
Singing the Jumbly Chorus still
As he sat all day on the grassy hill,

'Far and few, far and few,
Are the lands where the Jumblies live;
Their heads are green, and their hands are blue
And they went to sea in a sieve.'

But when the sun was low in the West,
The Dong arose and said;
'What little sense I once possessed
Has gone quite out of my head!'
And since that day he wanders still
By lake and forest, marsh and hill,
Singing, 'O somewhere, in valley or plain
Might I find my Jumbly Girl again!
For ever I'll seek by lake and shore
Till I find my Jumbly Girl once more!'

Playing a pipe with silvery squeaks,
Since then his Jumbly Girl he seeks,
And because by night he could not see,
He gathered the bark of the Twangum Tree
On the flowery plain that grows.
And he wove him a wondrous Nose,
A Nose as strange as a Nose could be!
Of vast proportions and painted red,
And tied with cords to the back of his head.
In a hollow rounded space it ended
With a luminous Lamp within suspended,
All fenced about
With a bandage stout
To prevent the wind from blowing it out;
And with holes all round to send the light,
In gleaming rays on the dismal night.

And now each night, and all night long,
Over those plains still roams the Dong;
And above the wail of the Chimp and Snipe
You may hear the squeak of his plaintive pipe
While ever he seeks, but seeks in vain
To meet with his Jumbly Girl again;
Lonely and wild — all night he goes,
The Dong with a luminous Nose!
And all who watch at the midnight hour,
From Hall or Terrace, or lofty Tower,
Cry, as they trace the Meteor bright,
Moving along through the dreary night,
'This is the hour when forth he goes,
The Dong with a luminous Nose!
Yonder — over the plain he goes;
He goes!
He goes;
The Dong with a luminous Nose!'

Edward Lear

The Night Will Never Stay

The night will never stay,
The night will still go by,
Though with a million stars
You pin it to the sky;
Though you bind it with the blowing wind
And buckle it with the moon,
The night will slip away
Like sorrow or a tune.

Eleanor Farjeon

Sam Groom

What are you writing down there, Sam Groom,
All alone in a deep, damp room,
Nose on the paper, tongue held tight,
What are you writing by candle-light?
    Words, says Sam.
    That's what I am.

Why do you write down there, Sam Groom,
While the bright bees buzz and the roses bloom?
Scribble and scrape goes your pen all day
As the sun and summer waste away.

Are you writing to your mammy or your daddy, Sam Groom,
Squinting your eye in the candle-fume,
To your brother or your sister or your own true-dove
Or a friend or a foe that we know not of?

Is it a sermon or a bill of sale,
A shilling-shocker or a nursery-tale?
Is it blank, blank verse or a tally of rhymes
Or a letter to the Editor of *The Times*?

Are you putting the wrongs to rights, Sam Groom,
As you sit in a kitchen as chill as the tomb?
Is it songs for the owl or songs for the lark
Or a tune to whistle against the dark?

They say that you'll stay where you are, Sam Groom,
From half-past nothing to the day of doom.
What are you writing down there, Sam Groom,
All alone in a deep, damp room?
    Words, says Sam.
    That's what I am.

Charles Causley

The Old Men Admiring Themselves in the Water

I heard the old, old men say,
'Everything alters,
And one by one we drop away.'
They had hands like claws, and their knees
Were twisted like the old thorn-trees
By the waters.
I heard the old, old men say,
'All that's beautiful drifts away
Like the waters.'

W. B. Yeats

The White Knight's Song

I'll tell thee everything I can;
  There's little to relate.
I saw an aged aged man,
  A-sitting on a gate.
'Who are you, aged man?' I said.
  'And how is it you live?'
And his answer trickled through my head,
  Like water through a sieve.

He said 'I look for butterflies
  That sleep among the wheat;
I make them into mutton-pies,
  And sell them in the street.
I sell them unto men,' he said,
  'Who sail the stormy seas;
And that's the way I get my bread —
  A trifle, if you please.'

But I was thinking of a plan
  To dye one's whiskers green,
And always use so large a fan
  That they could not be seen.
So, having no reply to give
  To what the old man said,
I cried 'Come, tell me how you live!'
  And thumped him on the head.

His accents mild took up the tale:
  He said 'I go my ways,
And when I find a mountain-rill,
  I set it in a blaze;
And thence they make a stuff they call
  Rowland's Macassar-Oil —
Yet twopence-halfpenny is all
  They give me for my toil.'

But I was thinking of a way
  To feed oneself on batter,
And so go on from day to day
  Getting a little fatter.
I shook him well from side to side,
  Until his face was blue:
'Come, tell me how you live,' I cried,
  'And what it is you do!'

He said 'I hunt for haddocks' eyes
  Among the heather bright,
And work them into waistcoat-buttons
  In the silent night.
And these I do not sell for gold
  Or coin of silvery shine,
But for a copper halfpenny,
  And that will purchase nine.

'I sometimes dig for buttered rolls,
  Or set limed twigs for crabs;
I sometimes search the grassy knolls
  For wheels of Hansom-cabs.
And that's the way' (he gave a wink)
  'By which I get my wealth —
And very gladly will I drink
  Your Honour's noble health.'

I heard him then, for I had just
  Completed my design
To keep the Menai bridge from rust
  By boiling it in wine.
I thanked him much for telling me
  The way he got his wealth,
But chiefly for his wish that he
  Might drink my noble health.

And now, if e'er by chance I put
  My fingers into glue,
Or madly squeeze a right-hand foot
  Into a left-hand shoe,
Or if I drop upon my toe
  A very heavy weight,
I weep, for it reminds me so
  Of that old man I used to know —

Whose look was mild, whose speech was slow,
Whose hair was whiter than the snow,
Whose face was very like a crow,
With eyes, like cinders, all aglow,
Who seemed distracted with his woe,
Who rocked his body to and fro,
And muttered mumblingly and low,
As if his mouth were full of dough,
Who snorted like a buffalo —
That summer evening long ago
  A-sitting on a gate.

Lewis Carroll

Torch

I want a torch with a handle
So I can beam a yellow disc against the sky
So I can play tiggy in the dark

A waterproof torch
So I can dive into caves below the sea
So I can light my toes up in the bath

A flashing torch
To warn away the smugglers in the bay
And send messages to my friend

A little torch
So I can hold it in my teeth and climb up trees
And shine it through my cheek to make it glow.

A head-torch
So I can be a miner miles below ground
Or a cyclops with a single blinding eye.

I want a torch
So I can shine it through my hand and see my bones
So I can light my chin to make my face a mask

So I can poke round all the corners in my room
So my hands can make a shadow-show on the wall

But most of all
I want a torch
So I can snuggle with it deep below my quilt
And read, and read, and read.

Berlie Doherty

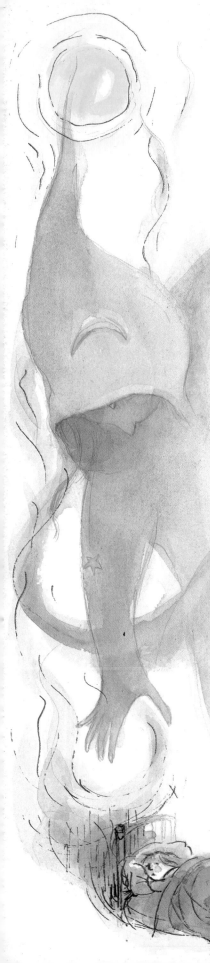

The Man who Steals Dreams

Santa Claus has a brother
A fact few people know
He does not have a friendly face
Or a beard as white as snow

He does not climb down chimneys
Or ride in an open sleigh
He is not kind and giving
But cruelly takes away

He is not fond of children
Or grown-ups who are kind
And emptiness the only gift
That he will leave behind

He is wraith, he is silent
He is greyness of steam
And if you're sleeping well tonight
Then hang on to your dream

He is sour, he is stooping
His cynic's cloak is black
And if he takes your dream away
You never get it back

Dreams with happy endings
With ambition and joy
Are the ones that he seeks
To capture and destroy

So, if you don't believe in Santa
Or in anything at all
The chances are his brother
Has already paid a call

Roger McGough

Bed Time

Can I stay up five
minutes more let me
finish this book
Can't I finish this
bead chain
Can't I finish this
castle
        Can't I
        stay up
five minutes or four
three minutes or two
minutes one minute more.

Accabre Huntley

165

Index of Titles and First Lines

Index of Authors

Index of Artists

Acknowledgements

The editors and publisher are grateful for permission to include the following copyright material:
John Agard: 'Ask Mummy Ask Daddy' and 'Cat in the Dark' from *I Din Do Nuttin* (The Bodley Head, 1991). Reprinted by permission of Random House UK Ltd. on behalf of John Agard. **Dorothy Aldis**: 'Little' from *Everything and Anything*, copyright 1925–1927, 1953–1955 by Dorothy Aldis. Reprinted by permission of Putnam Publishing Group. **Frank Asch**: 'Sunflakes' from *Country Pie*, © 1979 by Frank Asch (Greenwillow Books). Reprinted by permission of Greenwillow Books, a division of William Morrow & Company, Inc. **W.H. Auden**: 'The Night Mail' from *Collected Poems* edited by Edward Mendelson, copyright © 1938 by W.H. Auden (Faber/Random). Reprinted by permission of Faber & Faber Ltd. and Random House, Inc. **George Barker**: '"And what," said the Emperor', from *Collected Poems 1930–1955* by George Barker. Reprinted by permission of Faber & Faber Ltd. **Hilaire Belloc**: 'Matilda' from *Complete Verse* (Pimlico, a Division of Random Century). Reprinted by permission of the Peters Fraser & Dunlop Group Ltd. **Gerard Benson**: 'Three Birds' and 'Hlep' from *The Magnificent Callisto*, © Gerard Benson, 1992 (first published by Blackie Children's Books). Reprinted by permission of Penguin Books Ltd. **Edwin Brock**: 'Sally's Alphabet' from *Fred's Primer*. Reprinted by permission of David Higham Associates. **Charles Causley**: 'I am the Song' and 'Sam Groom' from *Collected Poems* (Macmillan). Reprinted by permission of David Higham Associates. **John Ciardi**: 'About the Teeth of Sharks'. Copyright holder not traced. **Stanley Cook**: 'The Performing Bag', 'Flowering Umbrellas', and 'Growing Cress in a Polystyrene Trough' from *The Dragon on the Wall*, © Stanley Cook, 1992 (first published by Blackie Children's Books). Reprinted by permission of Penguin Books Ltd. **June Crebbin**: 'The Whistler', 'Going Hairless', and 'First Day Back', © 1992 by June Crebbin, from *The Dinosaur's Dinner* (first published by Viking Children's Books). Reprinted by permission of Penguin Books Ltd. **Walter de la Mare**: 'The Ride-by-Nights' and 'Silver' from *The Complete Poems of Walter de la Mare* (1969). Reprinted by permission of The Literary Trustees of Walter de la Mare, and the Society of Authors as their representative. **Peter Dixon**: 'Teabag',

Oxford University Press, Great Clarendon Street, Oxford OX2 6DP

Oxford New York
Athens Auckland Bangkok Bogota Bombay
Buenos Aires Calcutta Cape Town Dar es Salaam Delhi
Florence Hong Kong Istanbul Karachi
Kuala Lumpur Madras Madrid Melbourne
Mexico City Nairobi Paris Singapore
Taipei Tokyo Toronto Warsaw

and associated companies in
Berlin Ibadan

Oxford is a trade mark of Oxford University Press

This selection and arrangement ©
Michael Harrison and Christopher Stuart-Clark 1995
First published 1995
First published by Oxford in the United States 1995
First published in paperback 1998

All rights reserved.

A CIP catalogue record for this book is available from the British Library

ISBN 0 19 276137 4 (hardback)
ISBN 0 19 276196 X (paperback)

Printed in Italy by G. Canale & C. S.p.A. - Borgaro T.se - TURIN

The All-Purpose Children's Poem

The first verse contains a princess
  Two witches (one evil, one good)
There is a castle in it somewhere
  And a dark and tangled wood.

The second has ghosts and vampires
  Monsters with foul-smelling breath
It sends shivers down the book spine
  And scares everybody to death.

The third is one of my favourites
  With rabbits in skirts and trousers
Who talk to each other like we do
  And live in neat little houses.

The fourth verse is bang up to date
  And in it anything goes.
Set in the city, it doesn't rhyme
  (Although, in a way it does).

The fifth is set in the future
(And as you can see, it's the last)
When the Word was made Computer
And books are a thing of the past.

Roger McGough